Hello, Beautiful!

Colorful Animals

WORLD BOOK

www.worldbook.com

World Book, Inc.
180 North LaSalle Street, Suite 900
Chicago, Illinois 60601
USA

For information about other World Book
publications, visit our website at
www.worldbook.com or call
1-800-WORLDBK (967-5325).

For information about sales to schools and
libraries, call 1-800-975-3250 (United States),
or 1-800-837-5365 (Canada).

Library of Congress Cataloging-in-Publication
Data for this volume has been applied for.

Hello, Beautiful!
ISBN: 978-0-7166-3567-3 (set, hc.)

Colorful Animals
ISBN: 978-0-7166-3558-1

Also available as:
ISBN: 978-0-7166-3579-6 (e-book)

1st printing July 2018

Staff

Writer: Shawn Brennan

Executive Committee

President
Jim O'Rourke

Vice President and
Editor in Chief
Paul A. Kobasa

Vice President, Finance
Donald D. Keller

Vice President, Marketing
Jean Lin

Vice President,
International Sales
Maksim Rutenberg

Vice President, Technology
Jason Dole

Director, Human Resources
Bev Ecker

Editorial

Director, New Print
Tom Evans

Managing Editor, New Print
Jeff De La Rosa

Senior Editor, New Print
Shawn Brennan

Editor, New Print
Grace Guibert

Librarian
S. Thomas Richardson

Manager, Contracts &
Compliance (Rights &
Permissions)
Loranne K. Shields

Manager, Indexing Services
David Pofelski

Digital

Director, Digital Content
Development
Emily Kline

Director, Digital Product
Development
Erika Meller

Manager, Digital Products
Jonathan Wills

Graphics and Design

Senior Art Director
Tom Evans

Senior Visual
Communications Designer
Melanie Bender

Media Researcher
Rosalia Bledsoe

Manufacturing/
Production

Manufacturing Manager
Anne Fritzinger

Proofreader
Nathalie Strassheim

Contents

Introduction

Welcome to "Hello, Beautiful!" picture books!

This book is about colorful animals. Each book in the "Hello, Beautiful!" series uses large, colorful photographs and a few words to describe our world to children who are not yet reading on their own or are beginning to learn to read. For the benefit of both grown-up and child readers, a picture key is included in the back of the volume to describe each photograph and specific type of animal in more detail.

"Hello, Beautiful!" books can help pre-readers and starting readers get into the habit of having fun with books and learning from them, too. With pre-readers, a grown-up reader (parent, grandparent, librarian, teacher, older brother or sister) can point to the words on each page as he or she speaks them aloud to help the listening child associate the concept of text with the object or idea it describes.

Large, colorful photographs give pre-readers plenty to see while they listen to the reader. If no reader is available, pre-readers can "read" on their own, turning the pages of the book and speaking their own stories about what they see. For new readers, the photographs provide visual hints about the words on the page. Often, these words describe the specific type of animal shown. This animal may not be representative of all species, or types, of that animal.

This book displays some of the many kinds of colorful animals that live throughout the world. Help inspire respect and care for these important and beautiful animals by sharing this "Hello, Beautiful!" book with a child soon.

Chameleon

Hello, beautiful
chameleon!

You are a panther chameleon.
You are a type of lizard that
can change your color!

You use your long, sticky tongue to catch a bug to eat.

Duck

Hello, beautiful duck!

You are a mandarin duck.
You live on or near water.

You are covered in feathers
of bright purple, green,
brown, and white.

Fish

Hello, beautiful fish!

You are a longnose hawkfish. You live in a colorful, rocky part of the ocean.

You have a long nose! There are red and white lines across your body.

Frog

Hello, beautiful frog!

You are a **blue** poison dart frog. You are a slimy animal that lives in water and on land.

You have skin that will hurt us if we touch you! Your bright color warns us to stay away!

Lizard

Hello, beautiful lizard!

You are an eastern collared lizard. You are blue and yellow with black rings around your neck.

Your body is covered by little pieces called scales.

You can run fast
on your hind legs!

Monkey

Hello, beautiful monkey!

You are a mandrill. You live in forests.

You are big. You have bright blue cheeks and a flat red nose.

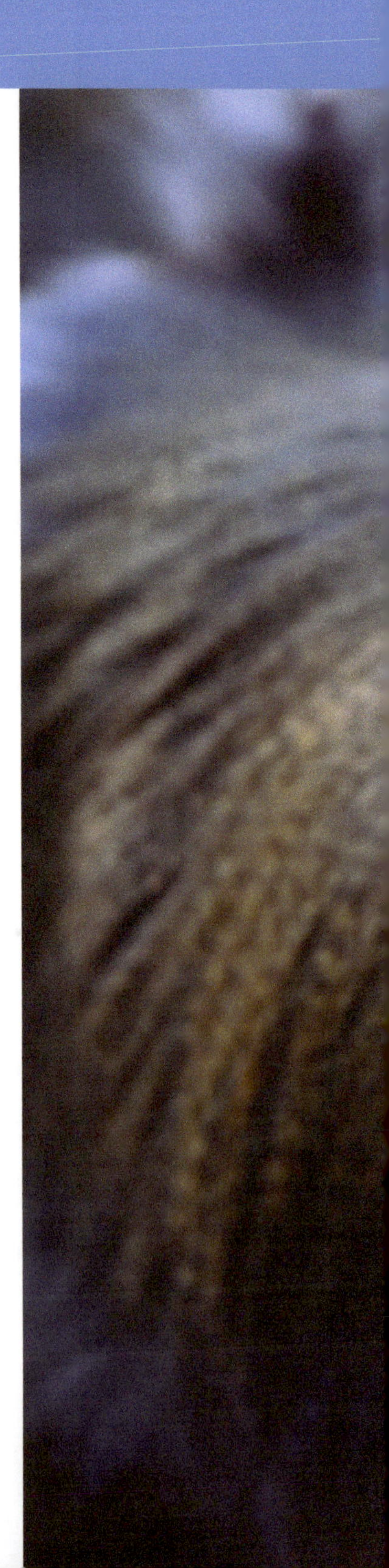

Moth

Hello, beautiful moth!

You are an elephant hawk moth. Your body and wings are **Pink**.

You looked like a tiny elephant's trunk before you grew into a moth!

Octopus

Hello, beautiful octopus!

You are a **blue-ringed** octopus. You have big eyes and eight long arms.

Your bite can hurt us!

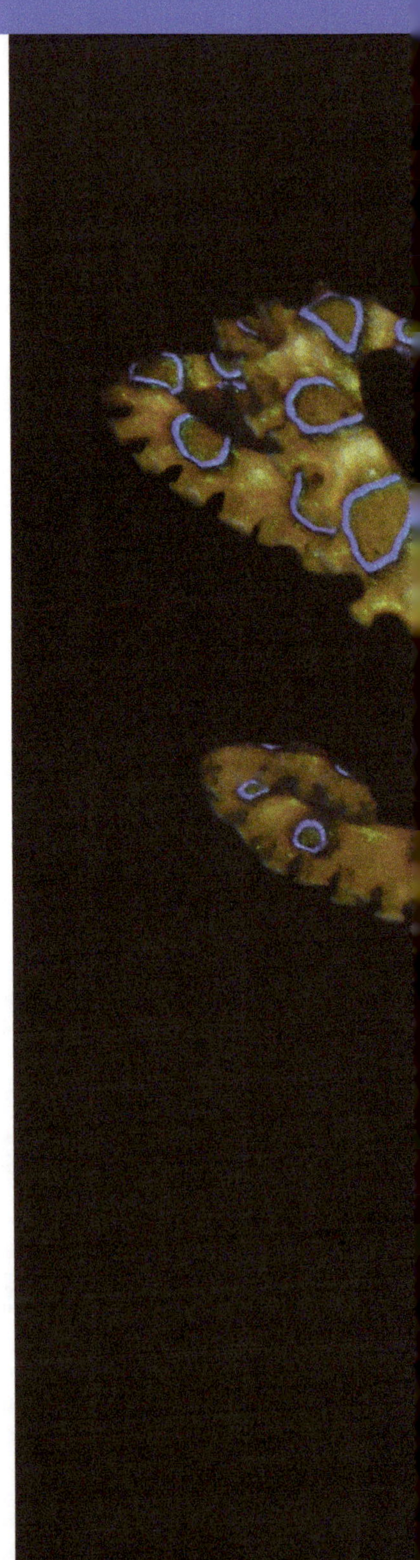

Parrot

Hello, beautiful parrot!

You are a scarlet macaw.
You live in warm forests.

You are a parrot with
a long tail and blue,
red, yellow, and
green feathers.

You fly high in the
jungle. You are noisy!

Snake

Hello, beautiful snake!

You are a rainbow boa.
You have a long body and
no legs.

You are a **reddish-brown**
snake. But in sunlight you
shine with the colors of
the rainbow.

Spider

Hello, beautiful spider!

You are a peacock spider. You have eight legs.

You like to dance and show your pretty colors!

Wasp

Hello,
beautiful wasp!

You are a cuckoo
wasp. You are a
small flying animal.

You are colored like a rainbow!

You may curl up
into a ball if
we touch you!

Picture Key

Learn more about these colorful animals! Use the picture keys below to learn where each animal lives, how big it grows, and its favorite foods!

Pages 6-7 Chameleon

The panther chameleon *(kuh MEE lee uhn)* lives in the forests of Madagascar, an island off the east coast of Africa. Males grow to 12 to 18 inches (30 to 45 centimeters). Females are much smaller. The panther chameleon primarily eats insects and other small creatures.

Pages 8-9 Duck

The mandarin duck lives in China and Japan. It is 16 to 19 inches (41 to 49 centimeters) long with a 26- to 30-inch (65- to 75-centimeter) wingspread. It eats mainly plants and seeds, but it will also eat snails, insects, and small fish.

Pages 10-11 Fish

The longnose hawkfish lives in tropical reefs in the Indian and Pacific oceans. It grows to about 5 inches (13 centimeters) long. It mainly eats tiny marine *invertebrates* (animals without backbones).

Pages 12-13 Frog

The blue poison dart frog lives in the southern part of the South American country of Suriname. Adult blue poison dart frogs range from 1 1/4 inches to 1 3/4 inches (3 to 4.5 centimeters) in length. They mainly eat ants, mites, and termites. They also eat beetles and millipedes. The skin of this frog is toxic to the touch.

Pages 14-15 Lizard

The eastern collared lizard is also called the common collared lizard. It is chiefly found in dry, open regions of the southwestern United States and in Mexico. It reaches 8 to 14 inches (20 to 36 centimeters) in length, including the tail. Eastern collared lizards eat grasshoppers, crickets, and other insects. They also eat other small animals, including lizards.

Pages 16-17 Monkey

The mandrill *(MAN druhl)* lives in the forests of the country of Cameroon and other parts of western Africa. Male mandrills are among the largest monkeys, weighing as much as 90 pounds (41 kilograms). Female mandrills weigh half as much. They feed on vegetation—especially fruits—and many kinds of insects.

Pages 18-19 Moth

The elephant hawk moth lives across much of Europe and Asia. It is a common moth in the United Kingdom and Ireland and has been introduced into British Columbia in Canada. It has a wingspread of 2 to 3 inches (5 to 7 centimeters). It feeds on the nectar of honeysuckle and other tubular flowers.

Pages 20-21 Octopus

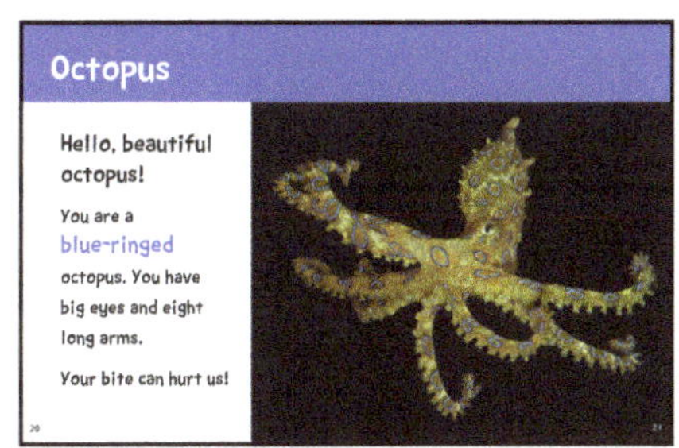

The blue-ringed octopus is commonly found along the southern Australian coast. Its body is about the size of a golf ball. They mainly eat small crabs and shrimp, but they will also feed on any fish they can catch. The bite of this octopus can kill a person.

Pages 22-23 Parrot

The scarlet macaw (muh KAW) lives in forested areas of South America, Central America, and Mexico. They grow to more than 30 inches (75 centimeters) in length, up to half of which is the long tail feathers. They mainly eat nuts, seeds, and fruit.

Pages 24-25 Snake

The rainbow boa lives in South America and lower Central America. Adults reach an average length of 5 to 6 feet (1.5 to 1.8 meters). They eat rodents, lizards, birds, and other small animals.

Pages 26-27 Spider

The peacock spider lives in parts of Australia. They are less than ¼ inch (6 millimeters) in body length. They eat insects, killing prey several times their size. A female peacock spider will sometimes eat the male if she is not impressed by his dancing!

Pages 28-29 Wasp

Cuckoo wasps live everywhere except Antarctica. Most are smaller than about ½ inch (1.2 centimeters) in length. Cuckoo wasps sneak their eggs into the nests of other insects. The young hatch and feed on the eggs and larvae (young) there.

Index

www.ingramcontent.com/pod-product-compliance
Lightning Source LLC
Chambersburg PA
CBHW041056050726
47599CB00018B/2167